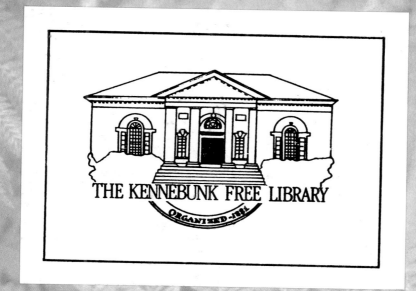

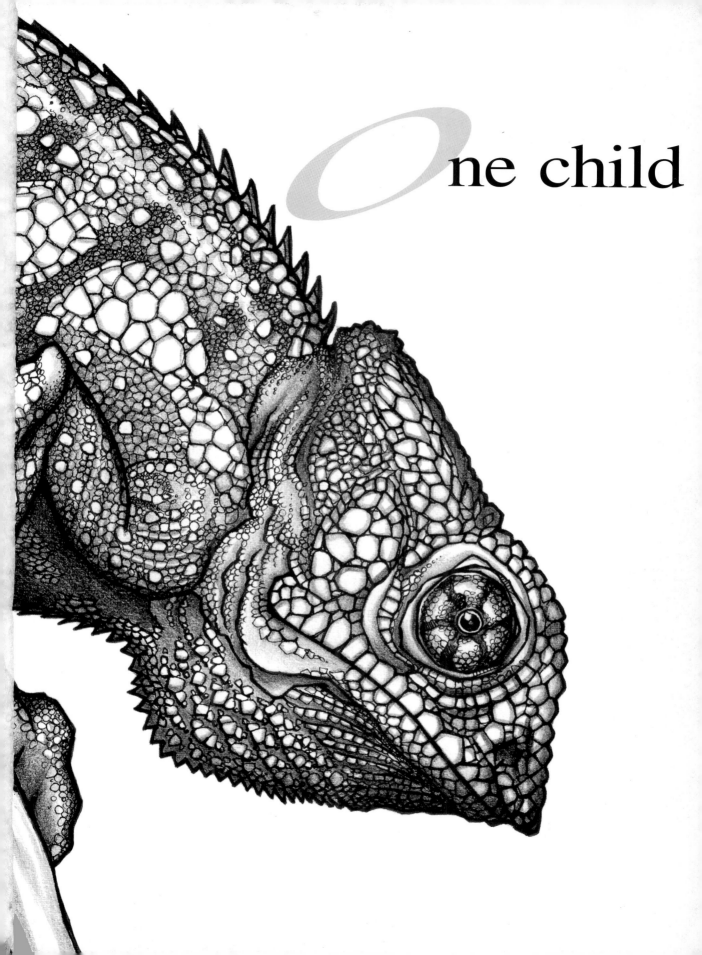

One child

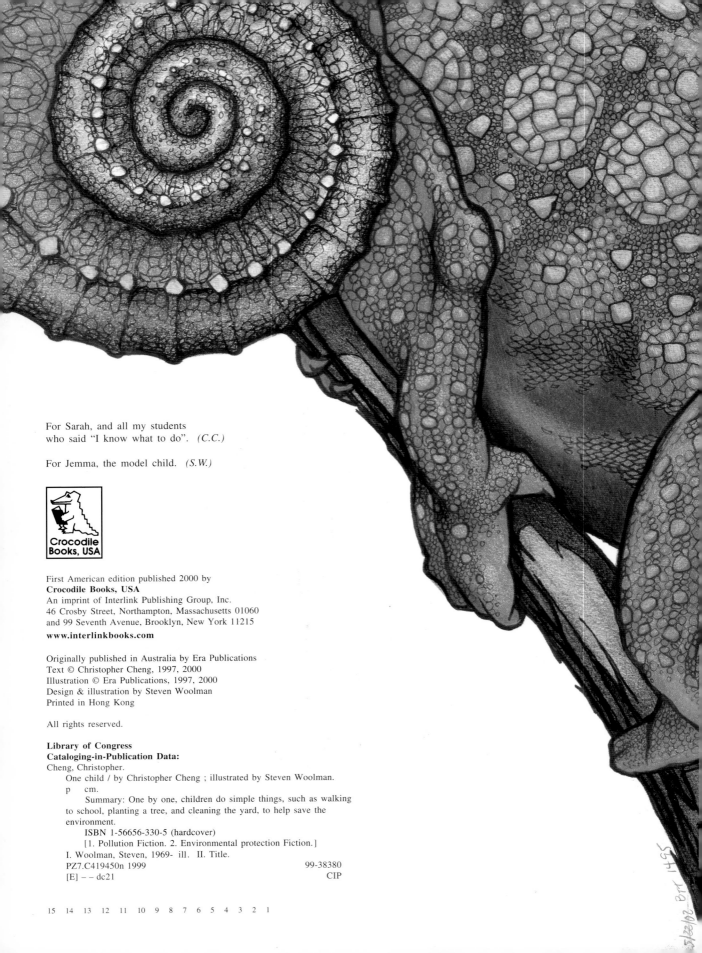

For Sarah, and all my students
who said "I know what to do". *(C.C.)*

For Jemma, the model child. *(S.W.)*

Crocodile Books, USA

First American edition published 2000 by
Crocodile Books, USA
An imprint of Interlink Publishing Group, Inc.
46 Crosby Street, Northampton, Massachusetts 01060
and 99 Seventh Avenue, Brooklyn, New York 11215
www.interlinkbooks.com

Originally published in Australia by Era Publications
Text © Christopher Cheng, 1997, 2000
Illustration © Era Publications, 1997, 2000
Design & illustration by Steven Woolman
Printed in Hong Kong

Library of Congress
Cataloging-in-Publication Data:
Cheng, Christopher.
      One child / by Christopher Cheng ; illustrated by Steven Woolman.
      p   cm.
          Summary: One by one, children do simple things, such as walking
to school, planting a tree, and cleaning the yard, to help save the
environment.
          ISBN 1-56656-330-5 (hardcover)
          [1. Pollution Fiction. 2. Environmental protection Fiction.]
I. Woolman, Steven, 1969- ill. II. Title.
PZ7.C419450n 1999   99-38380
[E] – – dc21   CIP

15   14   13   12   11   10   9   8   7   6   5   4   3   2   1

One child

Christopher Cheng & Steven Woolman

One child saw trees
   torn from the ground;
saw oceans stained with waste,
   no longer blue and clean;
saw skies choking,
   blocking the sun.

One child sighed and cried,
   "What can I do?"

One child saw animals killed,
 to be worn as coats and shoes;
saw fish floating in the river,
 gasping for air;
saw birds shot, just for sport.

One child sighed and cried,
"What can I do?"

then One child whispered,
"I know what I can do."

One child planted a tree.

One child walked to school

and cleaned up the yard.

One child wrote for the sea and sang for the sky

and marched for the animals
and spoke for the world.

One child did *all* that she could.

ust imagine if the children of the world did all that they could.

Imagine.

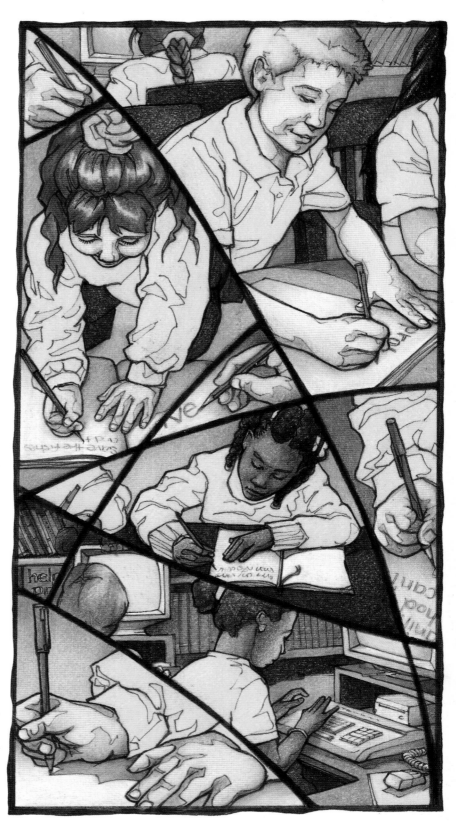

Imagine.

Just imagine.

2002
Treasures